The Day It Snowed Popcorn

By Teri Schure

THIS BOOK BELONGS TO

____

WITH LOVE FROM

____

ISBN: 978-1-62550-598-9 PB

978-1-62550-599-6 EB

Library of Congress Control Number: 2019914771

Printed in the United States of America

10 9 8 7 6 5 4 3 2 1

The Story of It

While reading *The Day It Rained Popcorn* to my two grandsons, Wes wanted me to tell him "the whole story of it."

So here goes.

I began writing the book in 1970 when I was seventeen, and then forgot about it.

In 1992, I discovered the unfinished adventure buried in some old files, and read it to my enraptured son and daughter, renaming the characters after them. In 2016, it became the go-to bedtime story for my two oldest grandchildren, and once again, I changed the names of the two main characters—this time to reflect theirs.

The reaction to the narrative first told more than four decades ago has always been the same. Those little ones nearest and dearest to me who delighted in the telling wanted more information about the characters, asked why there were no pictures, and wondered why the story had no ending.

I always meant to figure out an ending.

But it wasn't until Caleb and Wes honored me with their fascinated interest in the tale that I finally decided it was time. In April of 2017, my intuitive and insightful seven-year-old grandson, Caleb, thought the title of my book should be *The Day It Snowed Popcorn* instead of *The Day It Rained Popcorn*.

I explained that the name of the book was a perfect fit for the storyline, and not to forget that the title was forty-seven years old!

But Caleb persisted, explaining, among other reasons, that snowing fit the action better than rain. His brainy analysis broke it all down for me.

And the more I thought about it, the more I knew Caleb was right—thus, the title was changed to *The Day It Snowed Popcorn*.

This book is dedicated to Caleb and Wes. Without them, *The Day It Snowed Popcorn* would never have evolved.

The Day It SNOWED POPCORN

Once upon a time, Wes and his older brother, Caleb, were playing near a stream in the woods behind their house.

"Let's play Hide-and-Seek," Caleb suggested. "Go hide, and I'll try to find you."

"No way," Wes replied emphatically, his eyes bulging with fright. "I don't want to hide. What if you can't find me?"

"So I'll hide, and you seek," Caleb answered. Wes shook his head, shouting, "I DON'T WANT TO PLAY HIDE AND SEEK!!!!!"

"Okay, okay," Caleb responded with a sigh. "We'll play tag."

Wes was still agitated. "Tag is okay, but DON'T HIDE."

Caleb shrugged. Wes was always afraid of something.

As Wes chased after Caleb, trying to tag him, a fierce storm began to form overhead.

"It's going to rain any minute!" Caleb cried out, looking at the gathering clouds.

"I think we better get home before something bad happens," Wes said nervously, his face scrunched up in fear.

Caleb, being older and more mature, was sure that a storm was heading in their direction, and he tried to pretend that there was nothing to worry about. But that didn't stop Wes from being scared.

As Caleb and Wes ran through the woods, a streak of lightning lit up the black sky, and suddenly, the torrential rain, heavy winds, and thick fog were upon them. It was dark and dreary, and the wind was howling through the trees, knocking branches to the ground.

Wes was terrified, and Caleb was trying to figure out what they should do.

"We need a place to stay until the storm blows over," Caleb yelled to Wes as he fought his way through the wind, thunder booming around them.

Wes hesitantly pointed to a small opening where the stream seemed to end. "Does that look like a hideout to you?"

They hurried over to examine the opening in the rocks. It was a cave, partially overgrown with weeds and bushes that made it almost impossible to see inside. Luckily for Caleb and Wes, the hole was large enough for them to fit into comfortably.

"I don't know about you," Wes whispered, "but I'm scared."

Caleb reassured Wes. "Don't be silly; it's just a cave! And okay, it's a little dark inside. But it's better than being stuck out here in the lightning and thunder. Let's check it out!"

Wes wasn't convinced, but the storm was way more worrisome than the cave, so he agreed to follow Caleb inside.

The cave started out pitch black, and it was nearly impossible to see ahead of them, but once their eyes got used to the dark, they realized they had entered a long narrow tunnel.

"Look over there!" Caleb said, pointing. "See that bright light? There's probably an opening at the end of the tunnel!" He sprinted ahead to find out.

Wes was troubled and uneasy about wandering inside the damp and dreary cave. But he was determined to follow Caleb toward the brightness in front of them; despite his fears.

As they came closer to the light, they squinted their eyes against the brightness of the opening. Caleb broke into a run toward the brilliant light. Wes cowered behind Caleb, grabbing his shirt in fear. Caleb kept wriggling, trying to get Wes off his back.

They stepped outside, and then glanced at each other in astonishment. It was snowing, and a blanket of freshly fallen snow covered the ground.

And yet the countryside was a lush green and full of colorful fruit trees. "There's snow everywhere!" Caleb shouted out incredulously.

"But it's summer," Wes said, although it looked like snow to him too! They were both confused because it was July.

Wes bit his nails. "What if there are bad guys out there?"

As Caleb plowed into the thick blanket of snow, it made an unusual crunching sound.

Wes didn't move.

Caleb carefully scrutinized the waist-high snow, and then opened his eyes wide!

"This isn't snow!" Caleb hollered in wonderment. "IT'S POPCORN!!!"

Wes didn't want to miss this, so he gathered up his courage and joined Caleb.

They shrieked and giggled delightedly, as they jumped and rolled around in the popcorn. After a while, the boys took a break, and they shoved as much popcorn as possible into their hungry mouths.

They both agreed it was the best tasting popcorn they'd ever eaten.

All that popcorn eating made Caleb thirsty, so he began to look around for a place to get a drink.

"Look Wes! There's a weird looking river over there!"

Wes only wanted to know one thing. "Is it scary?"

"Not at all," Caleb promised Wes, and they headed toward the water. "Anyway, you're with me."

Wes was doubtful, but he followed his brother anyway.

As the boys approached a small bridge overlooking the swiftly flowing river, they were both spellbound by what they saw.

The liquid flowing quickly past them was bright red, chock full of floating cherries and boulder-sized ice cubes!

It was no surprise that Wes stayed behind while Caleb bolted to the edge of the river, scooping up the red substance in his hand, and slurping it into his mouth.

"It's cherry soda!" he proclaimed, grabbing a cherry by its stem as proof.

Wes shook his head in disbelief. "You should be careful what you drink. You might get sick."

Caleb waved Wes off. "You worry too much. Climb down here and see for yourself."

Wes warily followed his brother who was now running toward a bright purple trail. Caleb looked back at Wes just long enough to signal him to join in the fun.

The purple pathway was surrounded on all sides by popcorn. Caleb bent down, and to his amazement, he was able to pull off a chunk of the purple trail. Then he took a nibble of it and handed Wes the rest.

Wes covered his mouth and refused to take it. "It's grape-flavored fruit roll-up," Caleb mumbled while munching on the treat. Wes wanted nothing to do with it.

As they explored the countryside, they noticed an orchard of apple trees. As they got closer, they realized that the bright red apples were candied!

Caleb climbed one of the trees to pluck an apple for each of them, but Wes again refused to even take a bite.

While Caleb chattered to him that the apple was delicious and safe to eat, Wes pointed apprehensively at a bright yellow cottage in the distance.

Caleb munched on his candy apple as the two of them headed toward the whimsical cottage. Caleb was slightly ahead of Wes, who of course, stayed several steps behind.

As they got closer to the cottage, Wes lagged further and further behind. Caleb approached the little house, looking back at Wes and pointing to several large trees on either side of the front door.

Wes deliberately dawdled far behind Caleb, all the while studying the weighted down trees, full of brightly colored dots. Caleb reached up to a low-hanging branch and plucked off a handful of them.

Upon closer observation, he discovered they were gumdrops and immediately popped some into his mouth. He threw a green one at Wes, who guardedly smelled it and then took a teeny tiny taste before wolfing it down. Even Wes had to admit the candy was delicious.

Caleb picked another handful and jabbered away to Wes as he shoved gumdrops in his mouth.

Wes was trying to be brave, so he reached up and pulled a bunch of gumdrops off the tree for himself.

Unhappily, looking at the cottage, he just wanted to go home. "What if bad guys live in there?"

"Don't be silly," Caleb scoffed. "This place looks safe enough to me. Let's go see if anyone's home."

Just then, the door cracked open a sliver causing Wes to back away from the cottage.

When the door swung wide open, Wes ducked behind a gumdrop tree with his eyes closed shut. When he finally dared to look, he saw a beautiful girl, a little younger than him, standing in front of them.

She had curly brown hair pushed back off her face with a purple polka dot bow and was dressed in a purple sweater with a matching skirt. She held a wicker basket covered with a white and purple checked napkin.

"Visitors! I love company!" she exclaimed in delight. Smiling broadly, she invited them in.

Caleb did not hesitate for one second, but Wes slowly and anxiously crept from behind the gumdrop tree and then got close enough to the cottage to see inside without entering.

The inside of the cottage looked like their sister's dollhouse. On the kitchen table was a platter of piping hot donut holes topped with colorful sprinkles.

The young girl introduced herself as Hazel and popped one of the donut holes into her mouth.

They were shocked because that was their sister's name! Caleb told her that she even looked like their sister, while Wes nodded his head up and down in agreement.

When Hazel offered Wes some donut holes and showed him the freshly baked cookies that were in her basket, he finally stepped inside the cottage.

Hazel poured them each a glass of milk, and as they munched on their snacks, the boys had a ton of questions about their strange surroundings. Wes wanted to know the name of where they were.

Hazel explained that it had no name. It just was.

She had questions for them as well, like how they had gotten there. She also wanted to know how they planned on getting back to wherever they were from.

Wes knew that this was a bad sign. Because if Hazel didn't know how they were going to get back home, how would *they* know?

Hazel listened intently as Caleb told her about the storm, the mysterious cave, and the tunnel.

She looked at Caleb, confused. "Cave? Tunnel? There aren't any caves or tunnels around here," she informed them.

As they continued to describe what had happened, Hazel was lost in thought, trying to figure it out. "This sounds like something the goblins would do," she finally decided.

"GOBLINS?" Wes repeated, trembling. "THEY MUST BE THE BAD GUYS!"

Hazel tried to calm Wes down. "They're green, and they look mean, but they're not bad guys."

Wes wigged out and jabbed his pointer finger in Caleb's face. "GREEN AND MEAN? I am NEVER going to be able to sleep tonight thinking about those goblins."

Hazel maintained her claim that the goblins weren't bad guys. They were just lonely and wanted someone to play with, and they were probably behind tricking Caleb and Wes.

Wes did not want to play with goblins. He begged to go back to the cave as quickly as possible, so they could get home before dark.

Hazel wanted to know what dark was. Wes wanted to know how many goblins there were.

Caleb was amazed that Hazel didn't know about the dark. As he tried to explain it to her, she guaranteed the boys would never see this thing they called dark because, in her land, the sun was always shining. Caleb was taken aback, but Wes jumped up and down for joy, because he was afraid of the dark.

Caleb wanted to stay a while, but Wes knew that their mom would be missing them and tried to persuade Hazel to take them back to the cave.

Hazel agreed, but wanted to know what a mom was!

The three of them followed the purple trail, then trudged through the popcorn, past the cherry soda river, and back onto the bridge in search of the cave.

Caleb and Wes stuffed their pockets with popcorn in case they got hungry on the way home. But when they got to where the cave had been, it was gone! There was no trace of an opening. None.

Wes started crying. "The cave was here, and now it's gone! I'm afraid we'll never get home."

"Don't worry, Wes," Hazel said, feeling sorry for him. "My friend, Weezy, the Wizard, will know what to do."

Wes sighed. "Weezy? Please tell me he's a good guy."

Hazel gently patted him on the back. "You'll love Weezy." Wes was unconvinced.

She led them down a path surrounded on both sides with swirly pink and green lollipops. Wes didn't dare touch them even though lollipops were his favorite candy. He kept asking Hazel what he would love about Weezy.

Caleb yanked a lollipop out of the ground and ate it on the way to Weezy's, while Wes continued to bombard Hazel with good guy vs. bad guy questions.

They zigzagged along the lollipop path until they came upon a fantastical pink chalet. Caleb was pointing at the hedges and laughing hysterically. Even Wes forgot about his worries when they discovered that all of the surrounding shrubs were giant puffs of cotton candy.

Wes shoved some spun sugar into his mouth while Hazel used the large knocker on Weezy's bright pink door.

When no one responded, Hazel opened the door and stepped into the chalet, followed by Caleb. Wes hung back by the entrance, eyeing the surroundings.

"No, Wes, it's not scary," Caleb called out from inside.

"How did you know I was going to ask you that?" Wes asked.

Caleb shook his head in disbelief, while Hazel chuckled out loud.

Cautiously, Wes approached the front door and strained his neck to see inside, but refused to enter.

As Hazel yelled out Weezy's name, Wes couldn't help but notice the mess inside. There were books strewn everywhere, and bottles of colorful potions spilled on the floor. There was a large cauldron in the middle of the room, overflowing with green liquid.

Smack in the middle of the chaos, Wes saw a throne-like chair floating in mid-air and jumped back and away from the entrance.

Caleb circled the airborne chair, looking for what it was attached to, but it just hung there like magic. Hazel continued to call Weezy's name, and eerily, the throne began to lower itself to the floor. After it landed, the Wizard appeared. He was sitting on it.

Caleb rubbed his eyes and was, admittedly, a little frightened, but Weezy was just an old man and seemed quite harmless.

The Wizard hopped off the chair. "I have been experimenting with my disappearing potion," he said.

Weezy was tall and skinny with a long white beard. He was wearing a pink robe and a matching crooked pointy hat. In his hand was a sparkly wand, its tip flickering brightly.

Wes suddenly appeared at the front window, his face pressed flat against the glass, observing Weezy.

Now Wes had never seen a Wizard before, but he didn't think Weezy looked all that scary, so he mustered up some courage and headed back to the door, tiptoeing quietly inside, making sure to remain as close to the doorway as possible.

"Hazel, my dear, what brings you here today?" the Wizard asked affectionately.

She introduced Caleb and Wes, who was still hugging the door and explained their situation to Weezy.

Weezy approached Wes. "Having trouble finding your way home?" he asked kindly.

Wes stumbled out of the chalet shrieking.

"Nervous little fellow," Weezy observed while Wes howled, running around the cotton candy bushes.

Caleb spoke next. "We're lost, Weezy. You see we went into a cave to get out of the rain, and there was a tunnel and then an opening at the other end, but now the cave is gone. Nowhere to be found. We need to get home."

The Wizard continued to watch Wes having hysterics outside, while at the same time pulling on his beard. He finally spoke. "I think I know who might be responsible for this dilemma. But before I solve your problem, can we get that kid in here? He's going to wake up every creature out there."

Hazel and Caleb shrugged their shoulders. They both told Weezy there was no way they could get Wes to do anything he didn't want to.

Weezy raised an eyebrow, then lifted his magic wand and pointed it at Wes.

Poof! Wes was sitting in the chair inside the chalet bawling his eyes out and accusing Weezy of being a bad guy.

Weezy spoke quietly to Wes, reassuring him that he was not a bad guy and that he was on his team.

Although he covered his eyes with his hands the whole time Weezy was speaking, Wes eventually calmed down and peeked out, leaving enough space between his fingers to keep a watchful eye on things.

Once Wes stopped fussing, Weezy shuffled over to the laboratory table and pulled out a magnificent metallic blue box adorned with brilliant jewels. Wes uncovered his eyes a teensy bit more.

When Weezy opened the lid, swirls of brilliant colors floated around the mystical box. "Let's see if we can find out what happened to you kids."

Slowly the blur and mist of the churning colors began to take shape as a fuzzy image came into focus. It was a small creature with a green warty face.

Wes screeched and hid under the table.

"Gobbledy Goo, have you been up to your old tricks?" the Wizard inquired of the guilty-looking furry image peering back at him from the mist floating around the box.

Wes tried to pull Caleb under the table to protect him as he cried out, "I'm scared, I'm scared, I'm scared!"

While Caleb was pulling his leg away from Wes, Gobbledy Goo spoke to Weezy. "I'm lonesome. I want some friends. I meant no harm. I don't want to be scary. I want to play. I want to have fun."

His voice was high-pitched and squeaky. Gobbledy Goo wasn't scary at all, even though he did have a furry green face full of warts.

Wes peeked out from under the table. "Does that mean he's a good guy?"

"He's a pretty good guy," answered Weezy. "Gobbledy Goo was just looking for something to do. He would never hurt anyone. He's very kind. He's just a little funny-looking; that's all."

Gobbledy Goo looked hurt by the suggestion that he was funny-looking and then squeakily apologized to Wes and Caleb.

Wes came out from under the table to get a closer look at Gobbledy Goo.

When Gobbledy Goo saw Wes, he waved and smiled at him, and Wes smiled back. "He's not so scary," Wes confidently informed Caleb.

"Okay Gobbledy Goo, you need to send these boys back where they came from," ordered the Wizard.

"Not sure I can," squeaked the green goblin sadly.

"Hmmm," contemplated the Wizard. "We may have to call in the Flock."

Wes's wide eyes frantically darted from Caleb to Hazel to the Wizard.

Weezy stared back at Wes for a few seconds before saying, "No, the Flock isn't scary."

Wes was suspicious. "How'd you know what I was thinking?"

"Lucky guess," the Wizard responded, rolling his eyes.

Hazel spoke up next. "I'll call for the Flock," she declared as she dashed out the door. Wes hid behind Caleb as they followed Hazel outside.

"TICK TOCK, TICK TOCK, WEEZY NEEDS THE HELP OF THE FLOCK!" she bellowed out loud.

A few moments later, eight soaring birds swooped over the chalet. Wes looked at Weezy in terror. "Good guys," Weezy assured Wes, who breathed a long sigh of relief.

The birds were majestic and enormous, with long skinny necks, and white feathers with wing tips that looked like they had been dipped in black paint.

Each bird had a wingspan of at least ten feet, and the Flock landed gracefully and in perfect formation directly in front of Caleb and Wes.

Wes grabbed Caleb's arm tightly as the largest of the birds began to squawk-speak.

"We will take you where you need to go," the bird half spoke and half cawed. Two of the birds lowered themselves, beckoning the boys to climb on and ride them.

"No way," Wes stubbornly announced as he backed away.

Caleb replied by saying that if Wes didn't get on the bird, he was leaving him in this place with no name, no moms, and hideous goblins with yucky green warts.

Wes, realizing he had no choice, hopped up and onto the smaller of the two birds so fast, he almost slid off the other side. No way Caleb was going anywhere without him.

Hazel offered to fly with Wes, who was thrilled at her suggestion.

When Hazel jumped on his bird, sitting just behind him, Wes felt slightly safer. But he still kept his eyes shut tightly closed the whole time.

Caleb climbed onto the larger bird, and they said goodbye to Weezy and soared high above the popcorn fields, candy apple trees, and the river of cherry soda and bobbing ice cubes.

Even Hazel was in awe of the breathtaking scenery and urged Wes to open his eyes before he missed the whole thing.

"The only thing I'm missing is Mom and Dad," Wes replied. "So thanks, but no thanks."

Hazel wanted to know what a dad was.

Wes was too busy tightly grabbing onto the feathers of the ascending bird to answer.

Gliding and swooping in and out of the clouds, Caleb saw a giant, silver tube below them. He looked quizzically at Hazel who shouted that Weezy must have used his magic to conjure up a transport device.

Caleb was relieved to see that Wes still had his eyes closed. It was a no-brainer that this skyscraping tubular transport would give Wes a major worry attack.

They landed safely, and said their goodbyes to the Flock, waving as the majestic birds soared away.

Caleb, Wes, and Hazel gazed up at the imposing metal pipe towering over them. The sky-high steel contraption had a steeper-than-steep ladder attached to it. The tallest part of the winding tube plunged deep into a dark and ominous, gigantic hole.

Wes was jumping up and down, while hysterically repeating the same word over and over again. "SCARY, SCARY, SCARY, SCARY!"

Now it was Caleb's turn to be scared as he turned to Hazel, horrified, while Wes continued to scream and hop around.

Caleb was shaking all over and pleaded with Hazel to ask Weezy to come up with some other way for them to get home.

It wasn't easy, but Hazel finally convinced Caleb that the transport tube was the safest and quickest way to get them back home.

Wes had stopped jumping around, but he was hysterical and refused to climb the almost mile-high ladder. It took Caleb quite a while to persuade him otherwise.

It was only when Caleb started the long trek up the ladder himself, warning Wes that he was leaving with or without him, that Wes changed his mind.

He begged Caleb to come back down and promised that he would climb it, as long as Caleb protected him from behind.

The straight-up, thin metal ladder rattled both of them, but no one was more scared than Wes. He would inch up a rung or two and then scramble back down again. Caleb, right behind him, was petrified of falling, or being knocked off the ladder by his little brother, and kept urging Wes to move upward.

Eventually, the boys got to the top of the tube, with Caleb regularly poking Wes to move him along.

When they finally got to the upper part of the transport, Wes stood at the sizable opening, refusing to budge an inch. Caleb hung onto the ladder begging Wes to move over, so he could stand beside him.

It seemed like forever before Caleb finally convinced his little brother to jump into the tube. It wasn't until Caleb offered to go down alongside him, that Wes finally decided to go for it.

As Hazel gazed up at them from far below, they waved goodbye, held each other securely, shut their eyes tight, and plummeted down the slippery, twisty tube.

Wes shoved his head into Caleb's neck and just about burst his brother's eardrum from roaring so loud into it.

D O W N … A N D… A R O U N D … T H E Y … S L I D …..

Deep into the hole. Round and around, curving and twisting and turning...

U n t i l … P L O P! They landed right in front of their house!

They both lay flat on their backs, motionless, afraid to move. Caleb and Wes eyeballed each other in total amazement, but they didn't say one word and had no clue what to do next.

Then they looked around and realized that the transport tube was gone. And it was no longer raining. The sun was shining and it was a gloriously beautiful day!

Caleb looked at Wes, confused. "Do you think we were dreaming?"

Wes's eyes bulged. "No way. I would have been too scared to fall asleep in a storm," he declared emphatically.

"Of course, you would have been too scared," Caleb shot back wearily.

Wes defended himself, reminding Caleb that it took courage to climb the transport. And Caleb immediately and emphatically agreed, which made Wes proud.

As they went over what had happened, their mother rushed out of the house. She looked at both of them, relieved, while she angrily and repeatedly peppered them with questions about where they had been.

Caleb fibbed to his mother and said that they were playing Hide-and-Seek in the woods.

She eyed him suspiciously, knowing full well that Wes would never play a game of Hide-and-Seek, and then wanted to know why their pockets were bulging, requesting that they empty them out.

Wes and Caleb pulled them inside out, totally forgetting they were full of popcorn.

Mom scolded them for eating snacks without her permission and making up stories that they were in the woods.

She was certain that they had been next door at their Cousin Lila's house eating junk food the whole afternoon.

Cousin Lila watched from behind a tree, confused. She knew her cousins didn't spend the day with her.

The boys just shrugged their shoulders and looked down at the ground saying nothing, knowing that if they told their mother their story, she wouldn't believe a word of it.

They could hardly believe it themselves!

Their mother went back inside the house but not before ordering them to stay in the yard.

Caleb and Wes ignored her and barreled back into the woods looking here, there, and everywhere for the cave.

But it was nowhere to be found.

Caleb grabbed Wes's arm. "What do you think happened to us?"

Wes thought carefully about what to say, while Caleb waited for a response to his question.

Wes was thinking but had no explanation. He stared intently at the sky, as if the words he was looking for were, somehow, written there.

"Can I get an answer?" Caleb finally asked him.

"I am NEVER going to be able to sleep tonight," Wes replied, pointing his finger in Caleb's face.

AND THAT'S

The End

OF THE STORY.